PHILIPPINES

PAPUA NEW
GUINEA

ONESIA

Published by Goff Books. An Imprint of ORO Editions
Gordon Goff: Publisher
www.goffbooks.com
info@goffbooks.com

10 9 8 7 6 5 4 3 2 1

Library of Congress data available upon request.
World Rights: Available

ISBN: 978-1-939621-11-5

Color Separations and Printing: ORO Group Ltd.
Printed in China.
International Distribution: www.goffbooks.com/distribution

Designed by Sally Roydhouse Design
www.sallyroydhouse.com
www.findandseekbooks.com

FIND AND SEEK
SINGAPORE

2015: Celebrating Singapore's Golden Jubilee

A Gift from the People of Singapore

 NLB | National Library Board
Singapore

 Ministry of Communications and Information

 MINISTRY OF FOREIGN AFFAIRS
SINGAPORE

Written and Illustrated by **SALLY ROYDHOUSE**

goff BOOKS

We have finally arrived!

The airport is very busy.
I hold my mummy's hand tight.
People coming and going,
Airplanes taking flight.

Traveling down the highway,
Large trees tower along the side.
A lively city with sparkling buildings,
It's a spectacular sight.

First stop is the Botanical Gardens.
The thick air hugs my skin.
My scooter weaves through the paths,
Wet palms slap my legs and chin.

Faster and faster the wheels spin round, This time I decide to slow down.

I give myself a bit of a fright,

As Mum and Dad are out of sight.

Both appear around the bend at last,
Dad shakes his head, I flash a grin,
Mum tells me "Please don't go too fast",
"Don't get lost before we begin!"

槌柏水粿

加東榴槤
KATONG DURIAN

NO: 227 KATONG DURIAN

叉鸡鸡

The busy bustling hawker market,
Is a vibrant place to **eat**,
Rows of stalls and steaming pots,
It's difficult to get a seat.

I **hear** a lot of talking,
Words I haven't heard before,
Clinking bowls and chopsticks,
Smells waft across the floor.

I want to be brave and **eat** the food, noodles, dumplings, funny shaped spoons,

It's exciting to **taste**; it's fun to test,
Doesn't matter if you make a mess,

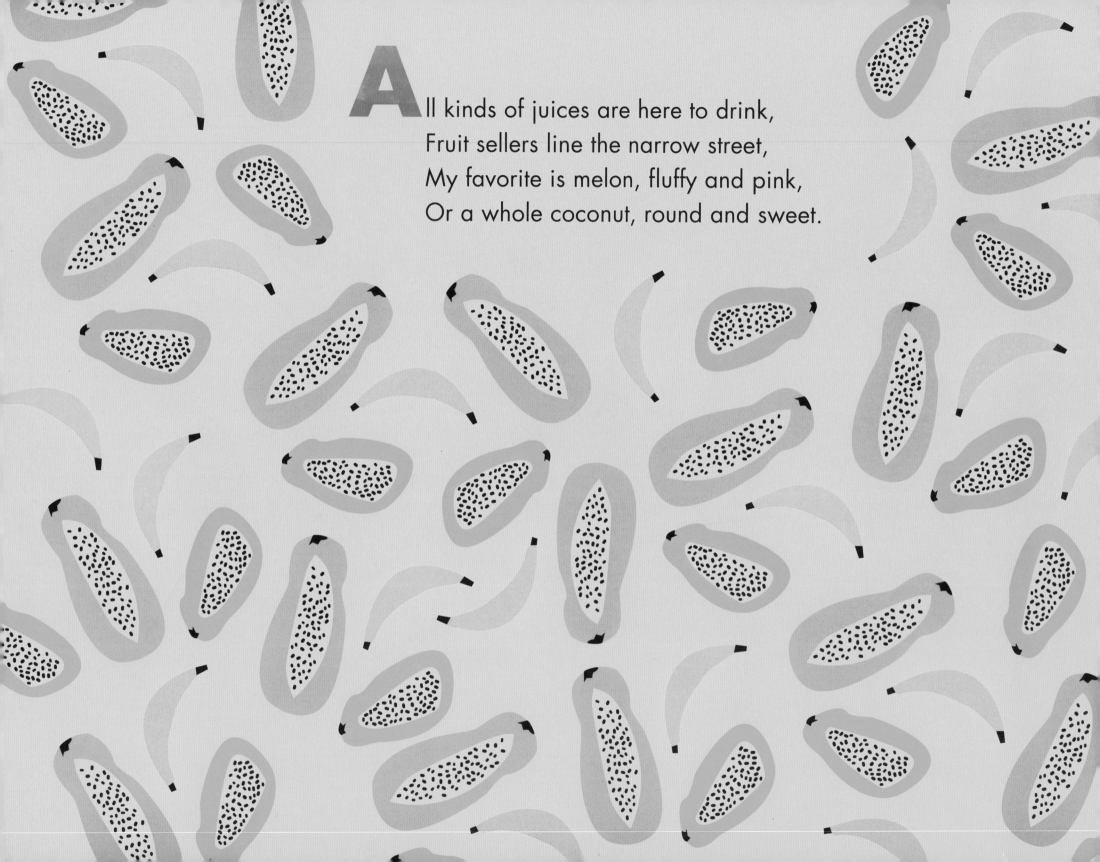

All kinds of juices are here to drink,
Fruit sellers line the narrow street,
My favorite is melon, fluffy and pink,
Or a whole coconut, round and sweet.

WATERMELON

PINEAPPLE

RAMBUTAN

So many bright colors,
Sticky fruit and juicy flesh,
Pierce them on your wooden sticks,
It *tastes* best when it's fresh.

TISSUES

CUT FrUITS

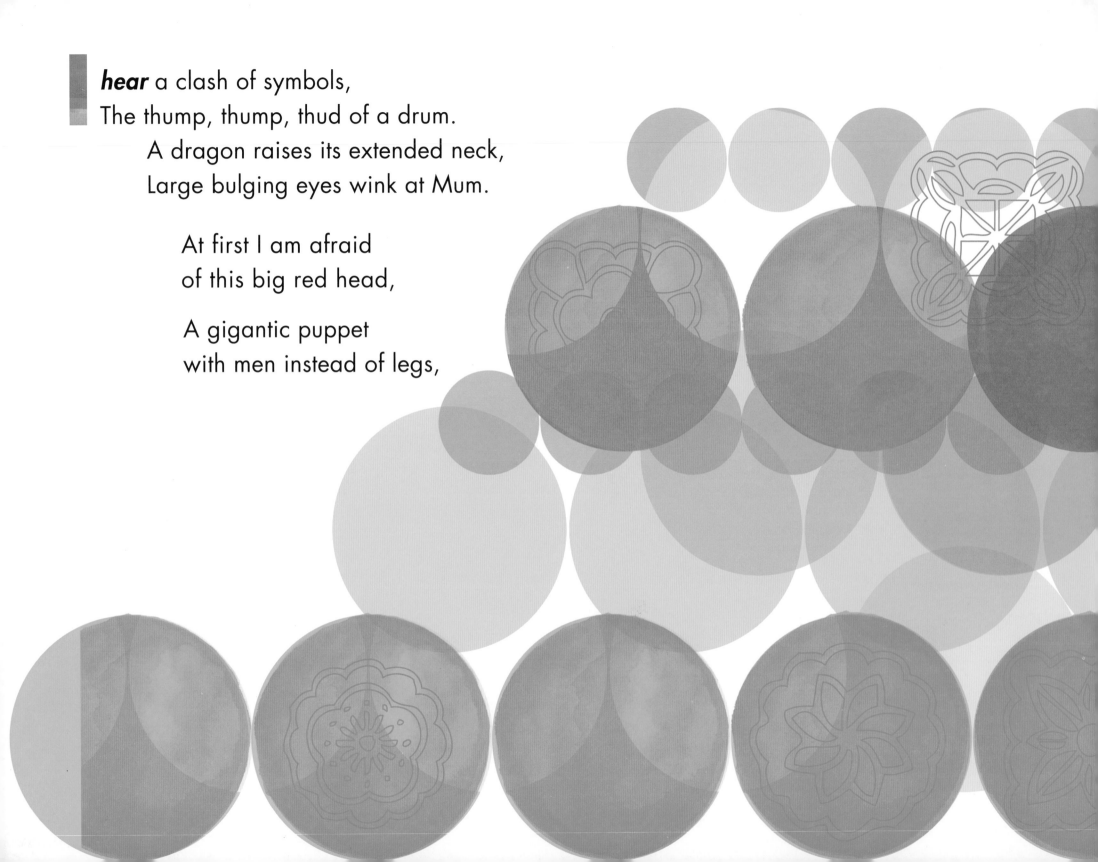

hear a clash of symbols,
The thump, thump, thud of a drum.
A dragon raises its extended neck,
Large bulging eyes wink at Mum.

At first I am afraid
of this big red head,

A gigantic puppet
with men instead of legs,

But all my fears disappear,
When I learn it is
Chinese New Year.

East Coast Park is a huge expanse,
Where I *see* the elegant fan ladies dance.

So graceful, delicate and in time,
Life stands still as their fans align.

At Marina Barrage another view rises,
Spectacular buildings of all shapes and sizes.

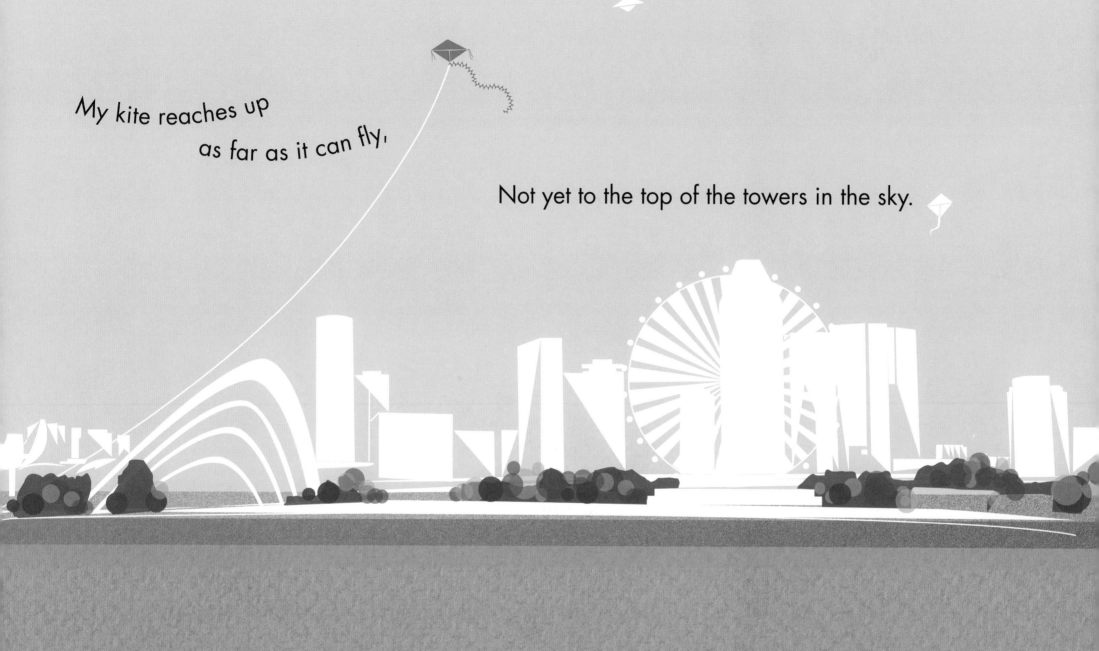

My kite reaches up
as far as it can fly,

Not yet to the top of the towers in the sky.

listen to the busy construction site,
And **see** the cranes stretch long and wide,

An ancient city evolving, ever changing,
And not yet finalized.

The zoo is a magical place,
A wonderland of fun,
Scales, feathers, claws or fins,
Every animal under the sun.

I ride on my dad's shoulders.
The view is great from up there.
Hungry eyes **look** back at me,
But I'm safe from any stare.

The sky above rumbles and tremors,
Thunderclouds split and balloon together,
Down fall droplets of rain coolness,
Relief from the heat, thank goodness!

Following comes a crack of lightning,
This can be very frightening.
A good traveller carries an umbrella,
To be ready for this kind of weather.

n a hot day we go to the aquarium,
It's cool and dark inside.
I **watch** schools of fish swim by,
And bright blue jellyfish glide.

hear the roar of a jet engine,
And feel the rumble in my chest,
I follow its trail across the sky,
The thunderous noise comes next.

I see the lolly colours of the shophouses,
And **listen** to the caged birds coo,
I wonder what goes on behind these walls,
Of pretty pinks, greens and blues?

Wouldn't it be fun to peak inside?
Just take a **look** and then quickly hide,
I know its not good to sticky beak,
But I'm curious, how do they speak?

Through the grand gate of a temple, Guarded by two protective lions,
Are **smells** of incense burning, Coils of smoke spiral and rise.

It's important to be quiet here,
Respectful of the traditional way,
Pictures on the walls tell stories,
Of spirits still worshipped today.

Water is my constant friend,
With humid days of very high heat,
There is nothing better than to splash around,
And **feel** the wetness beneath my feet.

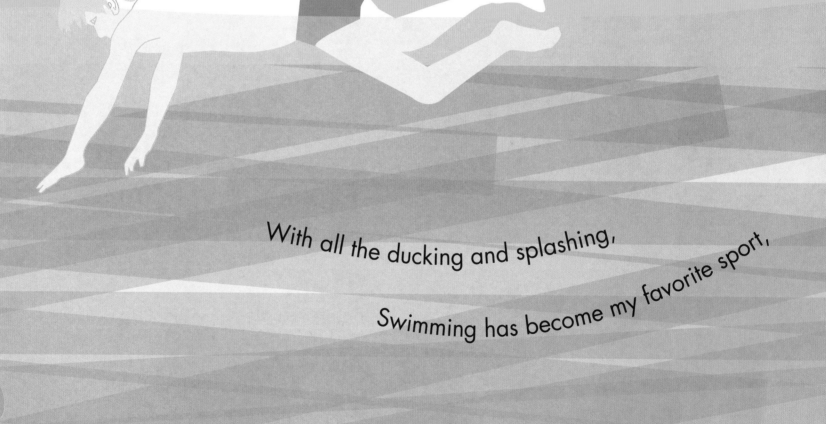

With all the ducking and splashing,

Swimming has become my favorite sport,

I have met so many wonderful friends
Who would have thought!

Through this adventure I have **seen** all types of things,
And discovered the happiness travelling brings.
Around the world, we all eat, love, and give,
These are the things we need to live.

The time has come to say goodbye,
To pack our bags and leave,
From fun days of adventure,
I have much in my memory to keep,

All kinds of people, places and experiences,
Singapore has been a treat.

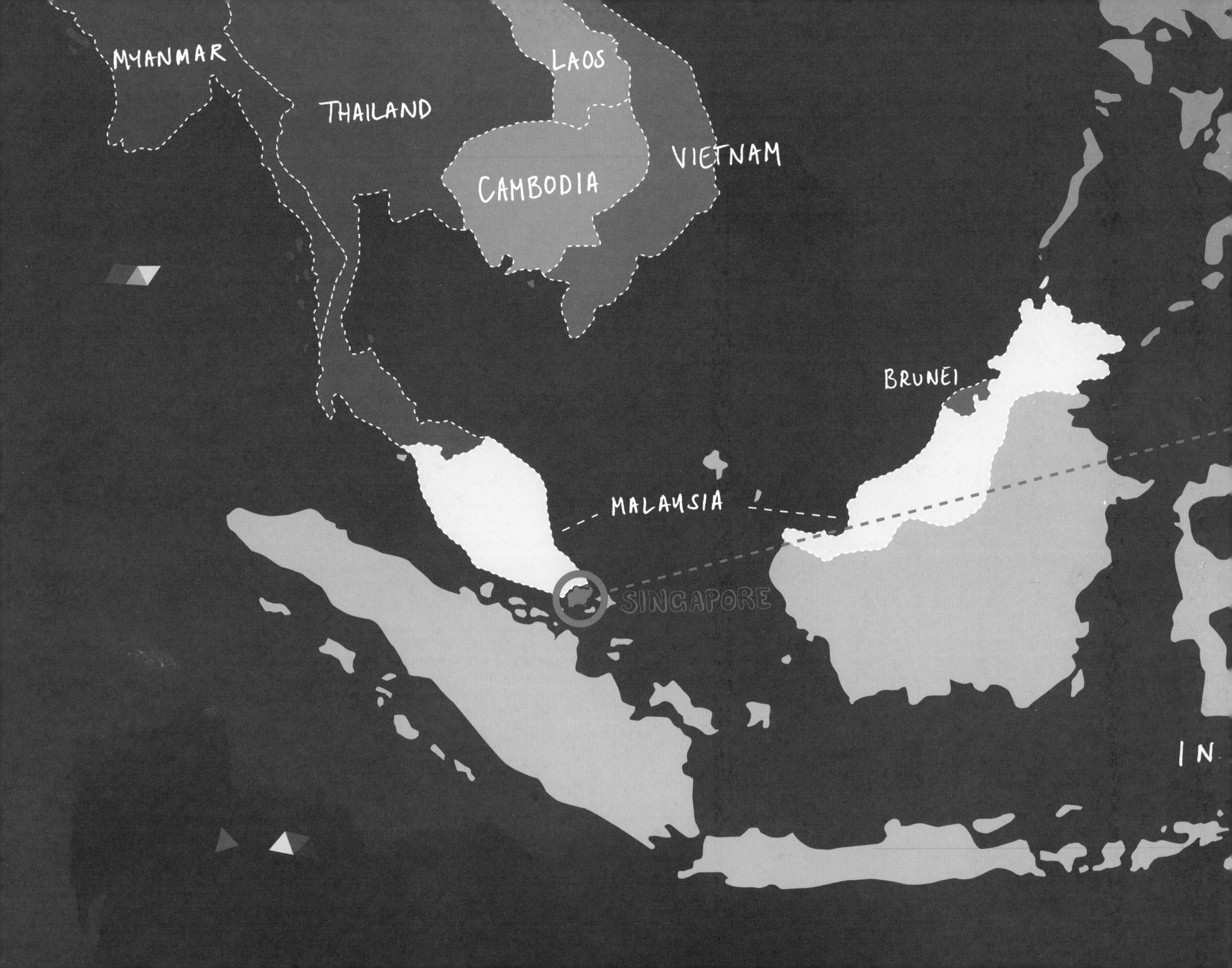
MYANMAR
LAOS
THAILAND
VIETNAM
CAMBODIA
BRUNEI
MALAYSIA
SINGAPORE
IN